What People are Saying...

"Everyday Worship's Scripture-packed, often witty, narrative is a must read for anyone wanting to know what the One we worship asks of our worship. Its friendly, engaging content also makes it an exceptional tool for worship leaders to use to create inspirational devotionals for their worship teams."

— Dr. Marty Trammell, Humanities Chair
Corban University
co-author of *Redeeming Relationships*
and *Spiritual Fitness*

"God has gifted Chris with an ability to share incredibly deep insights about our journey of faith, while using his great sense of humor to connect with us all like we're talking over a coffee at Starbucks. I would encourage any follower of Jesus to read this book and pray for God to give new insights into a deeper lifestyle of worship, everyday worship."

— Michael Bahn - Worship Pastor & Songwriter
River Valley Community Church, Grants Pass, Oregon

"What a simple and refreshing exploration of WORSHIP. The words on these pages are liberating - bringing both a seriousness to the privilege of worship, as well as a joy about the every day, every hour lifestyle of worship! God is truly deserving of all our praise and how great it is worship him in our every act!"

— Brian Heerwagen, CEO
DELTA Ministries International

Everyday Worship

Living to capture the heart of God

by Chris Voigt

Table of Contents

To Susan,

who believes I can conquer the

world for Jesus.

I FEEL A LITTLE LIKE AN OSCAR winner as they walk on stage with thirty seconds to thank everyone who's ever been a part of their project. It's impossible to remember everyone, let alone recognize them publically. I'm sure I will forget to mention someone who has been instrumental in shaping my story (consider this my apology ahead of time), and thus the story of this work. Nonetheless, I'm going to give it a shot, though in no particular order.

I have the privilege of working with an incredible team of pastors and elders at Dayspring Fellowship. Thank you for not just putting up with me, but also encouraging me, and giving me the freedom, to be the very best that Chris Voigt can be. Thank you, Dayspring, for letting me be a fool for Jesus up on that stage week after week.

To the Dayspring worship team: You rock! Most of what you are about to read came out of "Spiritual Direction with Pastor Chris," our weekly devotional time as a worship team. Your feedback has been inspirational.

Michelle, thank you for your constant encouragement and willingness to lend your question-writing talent to the end of every chapter.

Larry, thank you for being the iron that sharpens mine.

To my leadership team: thank you for praying, encouraging and working side-by-side as we live out these principles together. Aaron and Hur (you know who you are), words are not enough.

Ryan, I know there are more than four chapters and not enough pictures. Read it anyway! Otherwise you'll never know which part is about you. Thank you for being the Jonathan to my David (or am I Jonathan and you David? I can never remember).

Special thanks are owed to my friend, Lori, who has believed in me (sometimes more than I do myself) for ten years. She believed enough to spend hour after hour, reading and editing every draft of this book. You are a saint, sister.

Thank you to my parents and my in-laws. You have been an incredible blessing to me my entire life. Thank you for the love you show us. Thank you, Grandma Carol, (who is the grandma you will become familiar with in the pages to come). Grandma would want the rest of you to know that she doesn't buy into this Christianity stuff. That's OK, Grandma, we still love you.

To my children, Lexi and Josh: you are more precious to me than silver and gold (though I'd like to have a little of that too!). You inspire me to be the best dad and husband a man could ever be.

DeeDee, you are the best wife and life-partner a man could hope to have. I would be nowhere without you pushing, prodding and cheering me on year after year after year after year. You make me a better man.

WORSHIP IS COMPLETELY FOR AND ABOUT GOD. Period, end of story.

At the same time, the best worship integrates God's story into our personal stories. When the two come together, they weave a life-changing, epic saga that captures His heart, even as we surrender our own.

Contrary to common belief, music is not worship. Music can express worship, but worship exists independently of it. This book isn't about music. It is the story of how one man tries to model his life as an everyday act of worship. It is my hope that it might inspire you to do the same. That's why I kept it short and simple. So you'd read it. And with the help of some friends, I've included some questions for you to reflect upon to help you weave your own life-changing, epic saga.

I didn't write this work to impress anyone. It's not intended to be a theology of worship (although you're bound to find some). It will never be a best seller. It is a love letter from me to my Savior. My prayer is that you will become a worshiper like David, living to capture the heart of God.

Chris Voigt

April 2012

Chapter 1

Worship
is Our Purpose!

A S A KID I LOVED SPENDING SATURDAYS with my grandma. Saturday was always wash day, and with five sons and my grandpa, there was always a lot to wash.

What made wash day with grandma unique was her washing machine, if you could call it a machine. You see, grandma washed all of their clothes with a wringer washer. I loved turning the handle to help wring out the clothes before she went outside to hang them on the line. I'm not sure that I was much help, but grandma never complained that I was in the way. She only scolded me when I tried to put too much through the wringer and something got stuck.

I remember it was a big day when grandma got a new washing machine. It was a wringer washer with an electric motor. Now grandma was movin' on up. At the time, I never really understood why grandma didn't have a modern Maytag. Whenever I'd ask her about it she said "Why would I need a new washer when this one works just fine?" In fact, it wasn't until I was in college (the late 80s) that grandma actually bought a "real" washing machine and finally had time to relax a little on Saturdays.

Not long ago I asked grandma, "What invention has impacted society the most in your lifetime?" Having spent many Saturdays helping with the wash I was sure her answer would be the modern washing machine. I was wrong.

It was the refrigerator.

The invention of the refrigerator changed forever the way we shop, eat and store food. For a super-grandma like mine, who's spent more hours than we'll ever know growing and canning fruits and vegetables, food storage is a big deal. The fridge was invented for a noble purpose: to make life easier for people.

I admit a refrigerator has other potential uses as well. You could recycle it into the garden as an insulated planter. It could be used for storage. In *Indiana Jones and the Kingdom of the Crystal Skull,* Indy uses a fridge to store himself through a nuclear test (seriously, don't try this one at home).

Everything invented has a purpose...saving time, money, effort...or maybe to provide a little laughter. Did you know someone has "invented" powdered (dehydrated) water? Just add water and voila, you have water. OK, almost everything has a purpose.

Have you ever given any thought to *your* purpose? Why did God create you? What is your purpose?

And, are you fulfilling the purpose for which you were created? Or are you missing the mark, much like a refrigerator planter?

The cultural evidence – both inside and outside of the church – indicates that far too many people are still searching to find their purpose. We long for significance, rarely understanding that significance can only be found when we live the way we were created to live. Our search for significance can lead us on a wild goose chase. We look everywhere but the one place that

> **Significance can only be found when we live the way we were created to live.**

our deepest longings can be satisfied and our purpose can be discovered.

Fortunately, God didn't hide the answers from us. We need only look to His Word.

"16For by him all things were created: things in heaven and on earth, visible and invisible, whether thrones or powers or rulers or authorities; all things were created by him and for him." Colossians 1:16 [NIV, emphasis mine]

"6Bring my sons from afar and my daughters from the ends of the earth—7everyone who is called by my name, whom I created for my glory, whom I formed and made." Isaiah 43:6-7 [NIV, emphasis mine]

"11Furthermore, because of Christ, we have received an inheritance from God, for he chose us from the beginning, and all things happen just as he decided long ago. 12God's purpose was that we who were the first to trust in Christ should praise our glorious God." Ephesians 1:11-12 [NLT, emphasis mine]

"11You are worthy, O Lord our God, to receive glory and honor and power. For you created everything, and it is for your pleasure that they exist and were created." Revelation 4:11 [NLT emphasis mine]

> # We were created for His pleasure... created to please God.

I love this last one. We were created for His pleasure...created to please God. We were created to praise Him. We were created to worship.

Worship is hard-wired into the core of our existence. It's a part of our spiritual DNA. Throughout our lives we expend enormous amounts of energy – almost every moment, in fact – worshiping. (I guess you could argue sleep might be the exception.)

The question is never, "Will I worship?" but "What am I worshiping?"

For most of us the answer is "me". In fact, we are experts at pleasing ourselves, which would be perfect if we were created to be worshiped. Alas, we are not the boss.

I was hired for my first job when I was fifteen. I spent the summer stocking shelves, putting together lawn mowers and barbeques, and mixing paint at the local hardware store. My very first day on the job, they threw me to the wolves. The delivery truck had just come in and I had a whole section to restock.

There were thousands of packages I had to count, check off, organize and place on the shelves. It felt as if someone had dropped a glass vase on the cement floor and I had to glue it back together. I didn't know how fast I should go, or how perfect each shelf needed to look. I had never even heard of some of the items.

I didn't know many things. But I was sure about one: I wanted to please my new boss. I'd never live it down if I got fired on the first day. I knew that in order to be successful, I had to learn what pleased my boss. Just as I got it all down, the summer ended.

I don't know about you, but I'm pretty good at knowing what brings me pleasure: a nice house, nice cars, a picture perfect family, plenty of spare time, world peace and Diet Coke on tap in my office. I'm sure you have your own list.

That is the crux of the problem. Since the fall of man, we spend most of our lives running in circles trying to bring ourselves pleasure. We are always reaching for the next thing to satisfy our deepest desires. We look everywhere except the one place where we can truly find what we are seeking.

I guess the point here would be that it's probably not the things on my list that bring God pleasure. Unfortunately too few of us ever really try to figure out what pleases Him. Too few live their lives as an act of worship (our world would be a completely different place if we did).

We relegate worship to those few minutes of singing before the message in a church service and think we've fulfilled our obligation to worship.

If worship is all about bringing pleasure to God, and we want to be serious about worship, then we must understand exactly what brings Him pleasure.

We'll discover there is no checklist. Worship is not a list of rules to follow. If only it were that simple, that tangible. Worship is a living, breathing dynamic in the unique relationship that each one of us has with God.

Thoughts for Reflection:

1. What is your purpose?

2. What does worship mean to you?

3. What or whom are you currently worshiping?

4. Who are you trying to please? How?

5. What, in your life, brings you pleasure?

6. What, in your life, brings God pleasure?

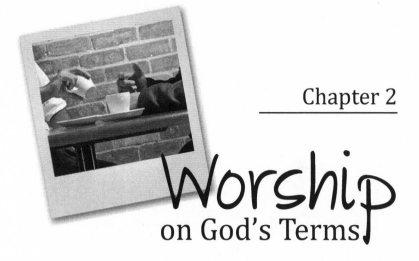

Chapter 2

Worship
on God's Terms

I LOVE DIET COKE.

I don't mean that I have mild preference for what type of soda I drink. I mean that I love to drink Diet Coke. Since a dentist's appointment in 1987, it has been my drink of choice. What started as a way to cut down on sugar, has turned into much more than just that.

I drink way too much every day. I am a purist so I choose restaurants based on whether or not they serve Coke products. I will drink the other diet cola, but only if I have to, and I feel like I'm cheating. I do drink other things, like water, frequently. However, when it comes to flavor, Diet Coke is the real thing.

A few years ago I started collecting Diet Coke cans from

around the world. I'd just returned from Italy with a Coca-Cola Light can and thought it was unique. Since then, friends have helped by bringing me cans from places like Dubai, Malaysia, Greece, Israel and other exotic locales. I have an original bottle of Diet Coke from 1983, the year after they started bottling it. I have a 25-year commemorative bottle.

My friend, Merle, even used his new lathe to fashion a wooden bottle of Diet Oak-A-Cola from a piece of spalted oak.

You might call my love of Diet Coke an addiction, or maybe an obsession, but I call it perfection on the rocks.

You can be honest. You have an obsession too. It might be shopping, sports, video games, or even Facebook. Something commands your attention and focus.

We have a tendency to think of an obsession as a negative thing. But we were created for an obsession. We just obsess about the wrong things. We focus on things that bring us pleasure. We should focus on the things that bring God pleasure.

In order to begin to understand what brings God pleasure, we're going to tackle what I believe is one of the toughest worship passages to understand.

We find this story in the second book of Samuel. The books of Samuel tell us some of the history of Israel as it transitioned from leadership by prophets, like Samuel, to kings.

A little background will help us understand the passage better.

When the Israelites left Egypt, years and years before this moment (which you can read about in the book of Exodus), God taught them what was required to have a relationship with Him. While they were in the desert, He gave Moses, the first leader of the nation of Israel, the plans for a tabernacle in which they would worship. He also gave him plans for all of the articles that would be needed in the tabernacle, including a chest that has become known as the Ark of the Covenant. Indiana Jones made the chest famous here in America.

I'm not sure that anyone really knows exactly what the Ark looks like because it has been lost to the public for more than two thousand years. It still exists, but it is in hiding, and there is much speculation as to its current location.

We do have a general description from Exodus 25. It was a chest that measured almost four feet long. On top were two cherubim facing each other with their wings meeting in the middle. It was overlaid with gold and had four golden rings – two on each side – big enough to slide poles through to carry the Ark.

To the Israelites, the Ark represented the presence of God, and was one of their most holy articles of worship. Wherever the Ark was, God was. In fact, sometimes they would take it into battle with them because they knew that if God was with them, they couldn't lose. Or so they thought. You'll have to read some of the historical account yourself to learn more.

King David, the second king of Israel, decided to make his home in Jerusalem. And logically, David, the most famous worshiper in history would naturally want the presence of

God close to him. So, in this part of the story, we find David in the process of bringing the Ark from Baalah to Jerusalem.

> *"¹David again brought together out of Israel chosen men, thirty thousand in all. ²He and all his men set out from Baalah of Judah to bring up from there the ark of God, which is called by the Name, the name of the LORD Almighty, who is enthroned between the cherubim that are on the ark. ³They set the ark of God on a new cart and brought it from the house of Abinadab, which was on the hill. Uzzah and Ahio, sons of Abinadab, were guiding the new cart ⁴with the ark of God on it, and Ahio was walking in front of it. ⁵David and the whole house of Israel were celebrating with all their might before the LORD, with songs and with harps, lyres, tambourines, sistrums and cymbals."* 2 Samuel 6:1-5 [NIV]

Imagine Times Square in New York City on New Year's Eve. This is the party to end all parties...it's loud, crazy, chaotic. The "whole house of Israel" means everyone, not just the 30,000 soldiers, came along to welcome God back to Israel. The presence of God is worth celebrating.

And then, in the midst of the celebration it says:

"⁶When they came to the threshing floor of Nacon, Uzzah reached out and took hold of the ark of God, because the oxen stumbled. ⁷The LORD's anger burned against Uzzah because of his irreverent act; therefore God struck him down and he died there beside the ark of God. ⁸Then David was angry because the LORD's wrath had broken out against Uzzah, and to this day that place is called Perez Uzzah." 2 Samuel 6:6-8 [NIV]

I read this passage, and there's a part of me that feels like this is unfair. Uzzah was only trying to help. He knew what the Ark represented. He knew its value to the entire nation. He was probably the only one out of the entire crowd of people who was even paying attention. Everyone else was lost in the moment. Without his help, the Ark would be laying on the ground, dirty and possibly broken.

Any reasonable person would wonder, "God, what in the world is going on?"

Let's go back to Exodus again. God's instructions to Moses were very clear. The Ark was to be moved by priests, who only came from the tribe of Levi. They were to carry the Ark using the poles designed to slide through the golden rings. It wasn't ever to be relegated to a cart drawn by oxen. It was holy, and entrusted to the care and attention of the priests alone.

Here is David's error. From the beginning of the journey they were disobeying the word of God. David made common that which was uncommon.

And then Uzzah compounds the problem. He was not a priest. He was a soldier. He had no right to touch the Ark, and he knew it. We are way off base if we ever think that God needs saving. We need saving, not God.

And this brings us to the heart of worship. David Peterson, in his book, *Engaging with God*, says: "Worship of the living and true God is essentially an engagement with Him on the terms that He proposes and in the way that He alone makes possible." If we want to engage with God we must do it on His terms. There is no middle ground.

God decides what is, or is not, worship. We have absolutely no say in the matter.

Worship on His terms means that we do it His way. According to the Westminster Catechism, dating

> God decides what is, or is not, worship. We have absolutely no say in the matter.

back to the sixteenth century, "The chief end of man is to glorify God, and to enjoy Him forever." If this is true then His way is to make worship our Holy Obsession. We should have a one-track mind. It should be all worship, all the time.

Most of us don't think of worship that way. We compartmentalize our lives and think worship is what we do when we come together as the church and sing. So if we aren't at church singing, we must not be worshiping. We fall into the trap of believing that worship is just about music and prayer and other churchy "stuff", and that what we do with the rest of our lives doesn't qualify as worship.

When you read through the Old Testament, you see that type of thinking was just as common then as it is now. And you find out how offensive this kind of thinking is to God.

Let's quickly look at three passages that illustrate what I mean:

In the book of Micah, we hear the words of the Lord as He indicts Israel for their trashing of their relationship with Him:

> "⁶*With what shall I come before the LORD and bow down before the exalted God? Shall I come before him with burnt offerings, with calves a year old? ⁷Will the LORD be pleased with thousands of*

rams, with ten thousand rivers of oil? Shall I offer
my firstborn for my transgression, the fruit of my
body for the sin of my soul? ⁸He has showed you,
O man, what is good. And what does the LORD
require of you? To act justly and to love mercy and
to walk humbly with your God." Micah 6:6-8 [NIV]

To put this in our terms: Should we come to church, sing, clap, and shout until we shake the earth, thinking it pleases Him then live our own lives, on our own terms, away from church? He has showed you, O man! We are to act justly, to love mercy and to walk humbly with God. To do this is worship.

In Jeremiah we find God, again, rejecting Israel for their rejection of Him:

"¹⁹Hear, O earth: I am bringing disaster on this
people, the fruit of their schemes, because they
have not listened to My words and have rejected
My law. ²⁰What do I care about incense from
Sheba or sweet calamus from a distant land? Your
burnt offerings are not acceptable; your sacrifices
do not please me." Jeremiah 6:19-20 [NIV]

Again, our offerings are made acceptable not just

because we give them, but because we listen to and obey the God we serve. Then our offerings are extensions of an authentic life of worship.

In this passage in 2 Chronicles, we find Israel preparing to celebrate Passover for the first time since Hezekiah restored the Temple:

> *"18Although most of the many people who came from Ephraim, Manasseh, Issachar and Zebulun had not purified themselves, yet they ate the Passover, contrary to what was written. But Hezekiah prayed for them, saying, 'May the LORD, who is good, pardon everyone 19who sets his heart on seeking God--the LORD, the God of his fathers-- even if he is not clean according to the rules of the sanctuary.'"* 2 Chronicles 30:18-19 [NIV]

Here we see that our perfection isn't what God requires. For the Israelites, it was a big deal to be unclean at Passover. Unclean people had to sit out Passover so you'd do everything you could to be clean. But to God it was more important to have a heart that seeks after Him. A seeking heart trumps outward cleanliness. A seeking heart equals worship.

In our hearts, we know that we are called to make our

worship a Holy Obsession. But our heads and the rest of our lives are in a constant battle to define what is acceptable to God. We take shortcuts and look for the easy way because 60 percent is better than most people offer, and as long as we rate higher in our comparison, we're safe...we're doing OK.

Unfortunately, the result is far less than the Holy Obsession we are called to make of our relationship with God. And we end up robbing God, and ourselves, of a deep, meaningful connection.

Thoughts for Reflection:

1. What currently commands your attention or focus?

2. Are there things in your life that keep you from whole-heartedly seeking God? What are they?

3. Is there any area of your life where you are "helping" God?

4. What are three new ways that you could worship God?

Chapter 3

Worship
is a Priority

N OT TOO LONG AGO WE PACKED up the kids and made our almost annual trek to eastern Oregon, where we go to visit family. The trip gives our kids, who are proper city kids, a chance to experience life a little differently, and us a chance to get out of the hubbub of a busy schedule.

Though visits to grandma's house no longer come with the joys of running clothes through the wringer washer, they are filled with other blessings.

Every morning grandma and grandpa get out of bed around 5:00 a.m. As she has almost every day for more than 50 years, grandma makes grandpa breakfast and they get started on their day. Around 8:00 a.m. the kids get up. Grandma, who has already cleaned up the kitchen from the first breakfast, lovingly makes breakfast for the kids, and then cleans up.

I get up around 9:00 a.m. Same grandma, same song... pancakes, hash browns, eggs, fresh fruit (strawberries if she can get them), orange juice and bacon. Lots of bacon, because grandma knows I love bacon. Don't even ask what time my wife gets up, but the same routine happens for her.

It's been that way every time I've ever visited grandma. She knows what each of us likes and makes sure that we get it when we visit. As much as I'd like to think it's only me who gets such incredible service, I know that she serves every person who walks through the doors of her home with just the same heart.

It's the same with dinner. Grandma knows that I love fresh turkey and cranberries. Not the store bought cranberries in a can, but the real thing. Even a summer dinner can be a full-on Thanksgiving meal, complete with foods cooked to the tastes of every person at the table. She even cooks a ham because grandpa isn't too wild about turkey.

As an expression of her love for those she cares about, grandma makes sure we are given a meal fit for a king. She could feed us anything and we would never know the

Worship is a Priority

difference, after all fast food is more common fare for us. To us, good grandma cooking is good grandma cooking no matter what she's making. But she would know the difference. What she makes reflects the state of her heart. To offer anything less than her best is not in her character.

As much as I love a fresh, Thanksgiving dinner any time of the year, I'm not too wild about leftovers. They usually just sit in the fridge until it's time to toss them. I know that seems weird to most of the world, but nothing can compare to a perfect meal prepared hot and fresh. Leftovers are a poor substitute for the real deal...even grandma's leftovers.

Some of you are appalled that I would speak so callously about leftovers. Cold pizza usually comes to the top of the list when it comes to leftovers. But really, you'll never convince me that cold, leftover pizza is as good as steaming hot, cheese melting all over the place, fresh from the oven pizza.

We feel that way about everything. We all want "new". We'll settle for used when we have to, and maybe even enjoy it and be happy and content. However, at the end of the day, it's "new" that we like. There's something about "used" that feels like we've settled for less.

God feels the same way about worship.

Malachi was an Old Testament prophet writing to the Israelites after they returned from exile in Babylon. Not only did they return from Babylon, but they also returned to their old ways.

They were sent into exile because they rejected the God who chose them. In the days of Malachi they were following that same path, making the same poor choices that got their parents and grandparents into trouble.

Malachi's message, sent as a warning call from God, confronted them about the sin they were embracing and called them back to their roots. Right off the bat, this is what God has to say about their worship:

> "*⁶Isn't it true that a son honors his father and a worker his master? So if I'm your Father, where's the honor? If I'm your Master, where's the respect?*" *God-of-the-Angel-Armies is calling you on the carpet:* "*You priests despise me!*" *You say,* '*Not so! How do we despise you?*' "*By your shoddy, sloppy, defiling worship.* *⁷When you say,* '*The altar of God is not important anymore; worship of God is no longer a priority,*' *that's defiling.*" Malachi 1:6-7 [The Message]

Them's fightin' words. God doesn't hold back, does He?

In any circus there is usually some clown with the ability to spin plates on the end of a long stick. Spinning one plate is cool enough, but as the act plays out, he keeps adding plates until there are almost too many to handle. He entertains the crowd by running to and fro as the plates wobble and sway, trying frantically to keep them from falling to the ground and breaking.

Like clowns, we spend most of our lives spinning too many plates, managing multiple priorities and other people's expectations. We try frantically to keep our plates from falling to the ground and breaking.

Our mistake is that we treat God like He is one of the plates.

When we do that, we downgrade God into the same category as little league, yard work and recreation.

As we've begun to see, worship shouldn't be one of our priorities. It should be our only priority, our only plate. Everything we do should flow from a life of worship.

Instead, we end up living like the priests of old, offering shoddy, worthless worship.

> *"⁸And when you offer worthless animals for*
> *sacrifices in worship, animals that you're trying*

to get rid of – blind and sick and crippled animals – isn't that defiling?" Malachi 1:8a [The Message]

Old Testament law required that sacrificial animals be perfect, without spot or blemish. In our urbanized, city-boy (or girl) life, we don't understand the significance of this requirement.

Perfect sheep don't come a dime a dozen. Most sheep have blemishes. There are more than thirty recognized genetic defects with sheep, from jaw defects, to eyelid defects, to undescended unmentionables. Even the color and quality of their wool can be considered defective. Perfect sheep are bred over many years and are incredibly valuable.

In her book, *Scouting the Divine*, Margaret Feinberg says, "When God asked for the sheep without blemish, spot, or defect, He was asking the people not just to hand over their best, but also to sacrifice something they had worked years to develop."

Offering sheep that were blind, sick or crippled was offensive to God. It was like offering Him leftovers.

I don't know about you, but I was raised to bring my best – my 'A' game – to everything I do. That doesn't mean everything is always perfect. I just do the best I can with the tools and knowledge that I have at any given time. Anything less is a reflection of my character.

> In our worship, we are called to offer our very best to God. Anything less is a reflection of our character.

In our worship, we are called to offer our very best to God. Anything less is a reflection of our character.

Maybe because we can't "see" Him we think it won't matter. Or, He won't notice. Or, out of sight out of mind. We just don't think of worship unless we're sitting in the pews, and we end up skimping on the portion we give to God.

"⁸Try a trick like that with your banker or your senator – how far do you think it will get you?" God-of-the-Angel-Armies asks you. ⁹"Get on your knees and pray that I will be gracious to you. You priests have gotten everyone in trouble. With this kind of conduct, do you think I'll pay attention to you?" God-of-the-Angel-Armies asks you. ¹⁰"Why doesn't one of you just shut the Temple doors and lock them? Then none of you can get in and play at religion with this silly, empty-headed worship. I am not pleased. The God-of-the-Angel-Armies

is not pleased. And I don't want any more of this so-called worship! Offering God Something Hand-Me-Down, Broken, or Useless." Malachi 1:8b-10 [The Message]

Or leftovers.

And because most of us live our lives with very little margin or space, all we have to offer are leftovers. We're tired. We spend our lives working, keeping our kids busy in sports and piano lessons, small groups, yard work, camping, video games, entertainment – fill in the blank with your distraction of choice. We fill every waking moment with something, and in the end we don't have any space or emotional energy to fit it all into the context of worship.

Worship gets shrunk down to the twenty minutes of singing we do when we go to church on Sunday (when we muster up enough energy to go), which we're in no frame of mind to enter into physically, emotionally or mentally.

The result is that we rob God of the honor due His name and ourselves of the spiritual refreshment that we receive when our life is oriented the way He intended. Our self-focused lives end up making worship more about us than Him. Not a wise choice.

"[11]I am honored all over the world. And there are people who know how to worship me all over the world, who honor me by bringing their best to me. They're saying it everywhere: 'God is greater, this God-of-the-Angel-Armies.' [12]All except you. Instead of honoring me, you profane me. You profane me when you say, 'Worship is not important, and what we bring to worship is of no account,' [13]and when you say, 'I'm bored – this doesn't do anything for me.' You act so superior, sticking your noses in the air – act superior to me, God-of-the-Angel-Armies! And when you do offer something to me, it's a hand-me-down, or broken, or useless. Do you think I'm going to accept it? This is God speaking to you!" Malachi 1:11-13 [The Message]

I'm pretty sure that very few people reading this actually think they are superior to the LORD Almighty. I'm just as sure that too many of us don't honor Him like we should.

As we continue on this journey we are going to dive deeper into what a life of worship actually looks like. But for now, think about the barriers that keep you from living as God has called you to live.

Have you been skating by, giving God leftovers?

Maybe you need to simplify your life so that you have the emotional and physical energy to connect with God more regularly? Are you connected to Him through His Holy Word?

To this point we've established a foundation for worship. God created us to glorify Him. He decides what does or doesn't bring Him glory. God expects the best of us, not what's left of us.

Now, let's figure out what worship actually is.

Thoughts for Reflection:

1. Do you have margin or space in your life or are you frantically "spinning plates" each day?

2. What will you do to build more margin into your life?

3. Identify any barriers, either good things or bad, which keep you from living as God has called you to live.

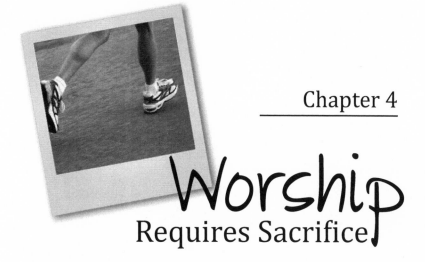

Chapter 4

Worship
Requires Sacrifice.

I'VE ALWAYS HATED EXERCISE. I've never thought of myself as all that athletic. I am a musician after all. Who cares which puck gets dunked into the field goal by the guy with the putter?

Calm down. I do know a little more than that about sports. I just don't like to admit it.

Childhood asthma made any sort of cardio downright dangerous for me. Just ask my doctor. I was always half-walking whenever we had to run cross-country in PE class. And don't even get me started on the Presidential Fitness Awards. What does running back and forth, carrying an eraser from one line to another prove anyway?

On the other hand, I do like french fries, with lots of salt and ketchup. From the bottomless steak fries at Red Robin to the sheer perfection of the fries from the golden arches, I am an expert on the fries of every fast food and chain restaurant on the west coast.

Unfortunately, they have yet to invent french fries that actually decrease your cholesterol.

Life was great. French fries and no exercise...until I turned 40.

It was at my "I'm getting old" physical that all those fries caught up to me. When they pricked my finger and canola oil came out, I knew it was time to change my tune. On a serious note, I knew that I really did want to live long enough to see my grandchildren. I need to be around to spoil them so I can get even with my children.

Fitness clubs give me the hives, so I knew I needed to find something I could do from home. Living in the land of Nike led me to running. Yes, I caved. I began to exercise.

When I started running, I refused to get all legalistic about any sort of set plan. I'm not a very competitive person, but I am pretty driven. In the beginning, I knew that if I gave in to the call to make every run farther and faster than the last that I would end up resenting every foot fall.

I gave myself permission to not compete against anyone,

myself included. I gave myself permission to change the plan mid-run if necessary. If I started out thinking I was going to only run for 20 minutes, but was ready to die at 15 minutes...I'd let 15 minutes be my goal. From the start I wasn't looking to run a marathon. Who has that kind of training time in their schedule anyway?

Unfortunately, exercise was only step one. Next...the french fries had to go...mostly; and, a bunch of other foods as well. I started keeping track of everything I ate. Again, not being completely legalistic. I don't count ketchup when I'm logging food; after all I'm not obsessive, or compulsive. But I am ruthlessly honest as I enter what I eat. Fortunately, there's an app for that.

Sometimes I've wondered if it's all worth it. During the past two years I've run more than 400 miles, a couple of miles at a time, two to three times per week. (Normal people should be impressed at this point. Serious runners... quit laughing).

It's inconvenient and time consuming. And although I've come to enjoy parts of it, the whole regimen is hard work. It takes discipline.

However, the results don't lie. According to my latest cholesterol screening I'm in great shape. My doctor and my insurance company are happy with me.

All things considered though, I wish I could have pressed the Staples Easy Button and gotten the same results.

It's OK to admit it. We're in the circle of trust. You feel the same way. We all do. Why do you think sales of lottery tickets are through the roof?

We live in a fast food culture that wants everything the quick and easy way. We've forgotten that everything worthwhile costs us something. Our insatiable hunger for faster, cheaper, better and free has left us allergic to discipline, sacrifice and hard work.

"What does this have to do with worship?" you might ask.

There is no quick and easy way to worship. Worship requires sacrifice. Let's take a look at an episode in King David's life.

Let's pick up the story in 2 Samuel 24. David had ruled for 40 years. Near the end of his reign, God tested him. God knew that something was off-kilter in his heart, and wanted to correct it.

> There is no quick and easy way to worship. Worship requires sacrifice.

So here's the scenario: David gives an order to Joab, his nephew and a general in Israel's army, to go out and count all of the people of Israel to see how many fighting men there were.

Joab knows that this isn't a good idea. He knows that it doesn't matter how many fighting men Israel has. Everything they have, every piece of land they own was given to them by God. If you've ever read the history of Israel you know they won some of the most incredible battles not because they were the strongest and mightiest, but because God was on their side. Do you know they won one of their battles just by playing some music?

But David is king, and kings usually get what they want, so Joab goes and counts. It takes more than nine months. And when he comes back and gives David the results David is overwhelmed with guilt and prays to God for forgiveness.

David is forgiven, but sin comes with consequences. David gets to pick between three choices: three years of famine, three months of being chased by his enemies or three days of an epidemic in the country.

David picks the plague because he trusts in the mercies of God. And get this...God lets loose an angel to spread the disease. He starts up in the northern part of Israel, in Dan and works his way down to Beersheba. The first day, from morning to evening, people get sick and seventy thousand die.

As the angel reaches Jerusalem, David looks up and sees the angel coming. David and all of the elders humble themselves and pray for mercy. And God stops the angel just as he reaches the threshing floor of Araunah.

Then, God tells David to go out to Araunah's and build an altar. David is quick to obey.

Araunah sees David and his men coming and goes out to meet them. When he finds out why David has graced him with his presence, he offers to give David not only his threshing floor, but the oxen for the offering and the yoke for the fire. He is after all the king. And Araunah knows that he lives or dies by the king's mercy.

What is astonishing is that David refuses the gift and instead purchases all of it from Araunah for a good price. His response is, "I'm not going to offer God, my God, sacrifices that are no sacrifice...sacrifices that cost me nothing."

I think we can draw three principles from David's experience and apply them to our worship today.

From a human perspective David didn't do anything wrong. He was king. He had every human right and authority to count the number of soldiers at his disposal.

In *humility*, David recognized that he had placed himself at the center of his tiny little universe. His turnaround moment came when Joab presented the numbers of fighting men in the country. We don't know exactly what triggered his change of heart, but I suspect that, in that moment, God reminded David of all of the battles he won when he was an underdog.

In Psalm 51:17, David says,

> *"The sacrifices of God are a broken spirit; a broken*
> *and contrite heart, O God, you will not despise."*
> [NIV]

Aren't we are just like David? We find security in a nice home, a fat bank account, a steady job, a lot of friends. We let these things edge God out of the center of our universe and they become the end rather than the means to bring Him glory.

In *surrender*, David submitted to the leadership of the God he served and accepted the consequences for his sin. Though imperfect, he was committed to following God – through the good or bad, whether deserved or undeserved.

It is easy to be surrendered when things are going well in our lives. How we handle the speed bumps along the way reveals the depth of our surrender.

All of this led to the *significance* he placed on worship. Worship requires personal sacrifice.

The concept of sacrifice was more tangible in biblical times. It made the cost easier to count. Go down to 7-Eleven and pick up a perfect lamb for slaughtering, throw in two doves and some grain for good measure and presto you have a sacrifice (it may have been a little more complicated than that. Don't quote me on the 7-Eleven part).

But even though the tangible "rules" of sacrifice changed through Jesus Christ, the principles of worship are still the same. God cares about the state of our hearts more than the cost of the cattle. Worship that is pleasing to God still costs us something...still requires sacrifice.

> Worship is not something we can delegate to someone else. No one else can worship for you.

Worship is not something we can delegate to someone else, or leave in the hands of the musicians in a church service. No one else can worship for you. It is your life, your character.

If David had accepted Araunah's gift, it would have been Araunah's act of worship, not David's. And in this case it would have been offensive to God, and would not have stopped the plague. You can delegate many things to other people, but worship is not one of them. And worship is not a part of some optional package when you sign on to Christianity. We are called to worship.

Thoughts for Reflection:

1. What does the statement, "Worship requires sacrifice" mean to you?

2. In what ways have you placed yourself at the center of your universe, rather than God?

3. What things get in the way of keeping God as your center?

4. What things might you need to surrender to God?

Chapter 5

Worship
is Enjoying God.

A FEW YEARS AGO WE WERE PRIVILEGED to enjoy two glorious weeks in Maui; arguably it is paradise on earth. For us, escaping the exile of the northwest in winter, with all of its clouds and rain, was a rare treat. Imagine being able to soak in vitamin D from the actual sun in the middle of winter. We were giddy at the prospect.

Other than sunshine, I didn't really know what to expect. I was born and raised in Oregon, so the only frame of reference I had for the ocean was our frigid piece of the Pacific. I don't particularly like to be numb from the cold so I was skeptical that I would really enjoy spending any time in the water. And, since I live my life on the go and don't just sit and do nothing very well, I wasn't sure relaxing on the beach would hold much interest for me either.

It didn't take long for me to join the ranks of body surfers, snorkelers and sunbathers. I think I am still finding sand in places you wouldn't want to know about. When we weren't at the beach we were sightseeing or shopping, and when we needed rest, we napped.

Our home away from home was located on the southern part of the island, on the border of Kihei and Wailea. Brewster House, a retreat for pastors and missionaries, is located on thirty beautiful acres –palm trees, mangoes, papaya, exotic birds and brilliant flowers – all overlooking the half-moon shaped snorkeling mecca of Molokini.

Our second floor balcony gave us a 180 degree view of the ocean to the west, and a perfect place to enjoy the sunset each evening.

After a satisfying day of adventure around the island, soaking up every minute of sunshine, it was magic to spend those last few daylight moments together. We watched the rays of light as they bent around the horizon to paint a beautiful canvas in the sky. Each sunset held just a few moments, when the sun had gone to bed, but the afterglow remained in the dimming night sky. It was almost as if the sun was longing for the day to go on, just like me.

It must be how Joshua felt.

The first time we hear about Joshua is in Exodus 17. Israel is attacked by Amalek, and Moses instructs Joshua to lead the fight on behalf of the new nation. He apparently captures the attention of heaven during the battle, and as a reward is singled out by God to hear that the battle was not in vain, that the memory of Amalek will be erased from heaven.

We don't know how Joshua earned his position as a leader. But from this point on, he is described as a trusted aide to Moses. Joshua has the privilege of being mentored by this great leader, chosen by God to eventually lead the Israelites into the Promised Land. He goes where Moses goes, sees what Moses sees, and has the unique opportunity to stand at the fifty yard line whenever Moses met with God, even on the mountain when Moses received the Ten Commandments (see Exodus 32:17). What a view.

In those days there was no question that God had chosen Moses to lead His people. The relationship the two of them shared manifested itself in very tangible ways, as God affirmed Moses' leadership to ensure the new nation would listen when he spoke.

On their roundabout journey from Egypt to the

Promised Land, the Israelites obviously lived a nomadic life. When God directed, they would pick up camp and move a bit closer to their destination. And, when God directed they would stop and set up camp again.

When they stopped, it was Moses' practice to set up a tent a ways outside of the camp. Pick up the story with me, beginning in Exodus 33:7 –

> *"⁷He called it the Tent of Meeting. Anyone who sought God would go to the Tent of Meeting outside the camp. ⁸It went like this: When Moses would go to the Tent, all the people would stand at attention; each man would take his position at the entrance to his tent with his eyes on Moses until he entered the Tent; ⁹whenever Moses entered the Tent, the Pillar of Cloud descended to the entrance to the Tent and God spoke with Moses. ¹⁰All the people would see the Pillar of Cloud at the entrance to the Tent, stand at attention, and then bow down in worship, each man at the entrance to his tent. ¹¹And God spoke with Moses face-to-face, as neighbors speak to one another."* Exodus 33:7-11a [NIV]

Imagine the holiness of those moments, the awe that overwhelmed the entire camp. Everyone worshiped. God was unmistakably in the house, and all eyes were on the glory of the God who had brought them out of exile; who had led them to freedom and was taking them to a land filled with milk and honey.

In every good alien movie there is a moment when the aliens enter the scene, and as people realize that something is about to happen silence begins to fall. People begin to focus on the creature and everything else just stops. It is so quiet for a moment you could hear a pin drop. Then mayhem usually breaks out.

I imagine that's what it would be like to see Moses move toward the tent opening. One by one, people would stop what they were doing as they realized what was about to happen. Silence falls over the camp. The sheep are still bleating, maybe a baby cries, but the sounds fade, unnoticed, as background noise. Everything but the tent fades away.

Then the physical realm gets a glimpse of the spiritual realm as God hovers over the Tent of Meeting to talk with Moses, just as you and I would talk as friends.

As the chosen nation of God you are witness to an historic moment, a life changing moment. To see the glory of God with your own eyes is beyond any experience anyone has ever had. No other god has ever sought a relationship with man (of course, how could they...they don't exist).

If you are Moses, this is as good as it gets. It's better than spending the day in paradise, bodysurfing and lying on the beach. You talk with God, argue about the stubborn people He's charged you with leading, solve world hunger, laugh at some antic from the day and say good night. God leaves and you go back to your tent to have dinner.

Joshua doesn't.

> *"11When he* [Moses] *would return to the camp, his attendant, the young man Joshua, stayed - he didn't leave the Tent."* Exodus 33:11b [NIV]

Joshua sticks around to enjoy the afterglow of God's presence. Like a picturesque Maui sunset, Joshua soaks up those precious few moments, after God has left, but the light of His presence lingers.

Joshua enjoyed the presence of God.

Joshua enjoyed the presence of God.

Now contrast Joshua's attitude with the attitude of the rest of the Israelites. Just a chapter later we find the people afraid of Moses when the afterglow of the presence of God lingered on his face. So much so that Moses resorted to wearing a veil to hide the glory of God. In a nation of around a million people, we only know for certain that Moses and Joshua enjoyed the presence of God. Sure, the entire nation was in awe of God. They were certainly afraid of God. But there's no evidence that they enjoyed being with God.

Which begs the question, "How do I enjoy the presence of God like Joshua?"

Joshua went wherever God was. From the mountain of God (where Moses received the Ten Commandments) to the tent of God, Joshua wasn't content to stand in the camp and watch from afar. He didn't want to stand on the sidelines, but in the game. When God showed up, Joshua maneuvered himself into the action.

Joshua stayed where God was. He wasn't in a hurry to rush off to the next thing. He was content to linger long after everyone else had forgotten that God had even shown up.

There are many places and situations where you can find God, if you are looking. Sometimes His presence will rattle the windows, but more often He is found in the gentlest of breezes.

The one place I know He can *always* be found is in His Word. Hebrews tells us that the Word of God is living and active. It's alive because God inhabits His Word.

If you'd like to start enjoying the presence of God, go to where He can be found. Start by getting into His Word. Regular reading, meditation, memorization and prayer through His Word will orient your heart to His presence.

Then, shut up. In our constantly connected, information overloaded world this can be quite challenging. We don't know how to enjoy silence. We're always surrounded by noise, and love the sound of our own voices too much to hear God's voice over the din. Quit telling Him what you want and spend time in silence letting Him fill the space.

This part takes practice.

And, linger. Rest in His presence. Focus your heart and mind on the moment. Forget about the unending list of priorities and tasks. Set aside the challenges in your relationships. The world will still turn while you stop to breathe in the presence of God.

In the spring I like to sit out on our front porch, enjoying the morning sun. I take my Bible, my journal and a Diet Coke. I sit. I rest. I fight the mental urge to do things. I invite Him to speak to my spirit. I enjoy the simple life of the

Worship is Enjoying God

occasional bird that dodges around the quaking aspen in our front yard. As the sun warms my body, I am reminded that it's warming pales in comparison to the warmth of the Son in my body.

Seek. Shut up. Linger. Learn to hear the voice of God and enjoy His presence in your life.

Thoughts for Reflection:

1. Do you respond to the presence of God like Moses, Joshua or the Israelites? Why?

2. Where do you find God? Explain.

3. What keeps you from lingering in His presence?

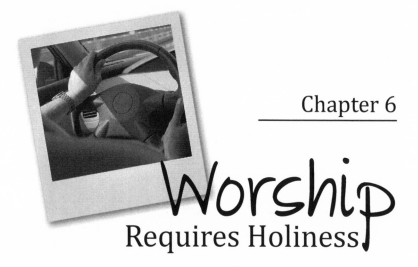

Chapter 6

Worship
Requires Holiness

I'M A FAIRLY LAW-ABIDING PERSON. I have, however, been the recipient of five tickets in my life. Two of them I should never have gotten. Yeah, you've heard that before. But let me plead my case.

First of all, I was on a mission trip doing God's work, and that alone should give me a pass. Second, I was innocent. I know. I know, everyone thinks they're "innocent", but in this case it's true. I had a police chaplain and a police chief fighting on my behalf. Even the Attorney General of the great state of Connecticut agreed with me and threw both tickets out. I was innocent, although I have avoided Connecticut ever since, just in case there's a bench warrant in my name.

For my third ticket, I was allegedly doing my crossword puzzle while hurtling down the freeway. Though I can neither confirm nor deny the veracity of that claim, if it were true, I would have, at least, had the common sense to put the paper on my steering wheel so I could keep my eyes on the road most of the time.

Now before you get all judgy on me, at least I wasn't eating my breakfast, shaving, texting home and watching a movie on my in-dash DVD player (that's right, you know who you are...I've seen you all driving)!

My fourth ticket came from Officer Friendly. Yes, that's what the ticket said. Officer Friendly issued a ticket, with a fine of $2999.99, for parking crooked in a parking space outside of a Shari's restaurant. Right. Officer Friendly may have lost his salvation for that one.

Most recently I actually got a speeding ticket. I was lost in my head, which is no way to drive, and was caught driving 38 mph in a 25 mph zone. Guilty as charged. The judge was so impressed I admitted it that he gave me the minimum fine and used me as a good example in front of the entire courtroom.

Normally I'm not much of a speeder, give or take a few miles per hour. But that didn't used to be true. Before

I bought a car with cruise control I was all over the map when it came to speed.

Have you ever noticed how it works? You're driving five mph over the limit because it feels better and no officer will stop you for that small of an infraction, which makes it seem like it's not really against the law anyway. Isn't it only illegal if you get caught? You'd be surprised at how many Christians I've talked to who believe that.

So, you're cruising along at 60 in a 55 mph zone. What happens when you come upon somebody actually doing the speed limit? Do you ever say, "Wow, I should slow down?" Of course not. More than likely you get a little frustrated that someone is in your way. Aren't they even paying attention to the flow of traffic? The slow lane is on the right, people. It's passing time again.

And you're driving 63 mph, not really paying attention to the speedometer when you race up behind another driver. "What are they thinking?" you ask yourself. "This isn't a Sunday drive through the country, grandpa."

As you fly by them, you turn and give them the look. You know the one. And now you're driving 67 and it feels like you're making decent time, finally. The cycle continues until you look down at your dash and notice how fast you are actually driving. And you feel a little guilty. When you finally slow down from 72 mph to 63 mph it feels like you're doing 40 mph and at that rate, you'll never get where you're going.

This is exactly how sin works. Sin has a voracious appetite. It is never satisfied. The more you feed it, the hungrier it gets. Just like teenaged boys. The faster you go, the faster you want to go. That's how we get sucked into the swirling vortex that seeks to destroy our lives.

No one ever just wakes up in the morning thinking, "I believe I'll destroy my life as I know it today by cheating on my spouse to fill the empty void in my life." An affair begins with disconnection at home, an innocent lunch, a passing touch, the stroke of an ego, laughter instead of rolled eyes.

It happens five miles an hour at a time, until the heart is entangled in a sticky web of lies, emotions and desires. Five miles an hour at a time until our need for "happiness" eclipses everything we believe, everyone to whom we are responsible.

It's not just the *big* sins that work this way. All sin works this way. All sin has an appetite. All sin seeks to be fed, and The Enemy knows how to lull us to sleep while we're making the journey. Look at how TV and movies have changed during the past twenty years. What used to be rated R is now PG-13. It all changed one bad word at a time, one titillating "love" scene at a time. Sometimes it's embarrassing how far we have gone.

Think of it this way. Pictured here is a printer's grayscale. A grayscale measures intensity, starting from pure white to total black with varying shades of gray in between. It's a perfect illustration for the appetite of sin. We get from white to black one step at a time – five miles an hour.

Sin is incompatible with worship.

> We must have a single-minded focus to do things God's way all the time.

If God calls us to make worship a holy obsession, we must have a single-minded focus to do things God's way all the time. You can't have a holy obsession without holiness.

The beauty is that, because of Jesus, God sees us as holy, regardless of any of our actions. We were justified on the cross. For us the question should never be "How does God see me?" He sees us as holy.

But sanctification is also a process, the process of becoming holy; which changes the question from "How does God see me?" to "How does God call me to live, to respond to what He's done in my life?"

And as worshipers, this question is of the utmost importance because the answer determines the quality of our worship. If worship is primarily a spiritual act, then the state of our spiritual lives determines the quality of our worship.

> **If worship is primarily a spiritual act, then the state of our spiritual lives determines the quality of our worship.**

Since most of us don't really embrace the process of holiness, we live somewhere in a shade of gray. Hopefully more gray than black, but not always.

God calls us to live differently than this. He calls us to be "pure white." He calls us to be holy. He calls us to be "set apart", which is the definition of holiness. The problem is that we live in this mess of a broken world that constantly fights against the values we claim to live by. We find ourselves living in some shade of gray and before long, we get comfortable.

And since we want to feel good about ourselves, rather than feeling guilty, we play the comparison game, because it is incredibly subjective and easy to make ourselves look good. You know the one, it begins with the sentence: "Well at least I'm better than ____." You fill in the blank. It may not be as obvious as this, but every time we stand in judgment of someone else that's what we're doing. We're basically saying, "I may not be perfect, I may be 50 percent gray, but look at them...they're at 70 percent. So I'm doing OK."

How then shall we live? Since none of us is perfect can we ever really be set apart? What does being set apart look like from God's perspective?

If we look to the book of Ezekiel, we find a picture of how God sees holiness with regards to us.

Ezekiel was a priest and prophet, living 600 years before Christ. He lived in a time of upheaval for the nations of Israel and Judah, nations taken into captivity by Babylon. As one of the captives, he wrote most of his prophecies from Babylon. One of the key themes of Ezekiel was the holiness of God and how it contrasted with the sin of the people of God.

The nations of Israel and Judah had allowed rampant sin to chase away the holiness God desired from them. They drank the Kool-Aid of the surrounding nations. In fact, Ezekiel tells us that the Israelites became worse than the other nations. They weren't just drinking the Kool-Aid of others; they were making their own Kool-Aid and giving it away for free.

It was so bad that they weren't just worshiping idols in their homes or in the town square. They allowed their sin to invade the Holy Temple of God. They actually drove God from His earthly domain.

And, when God couldn't stand it anymore, He brought judgment on them all, including the destruction of the Temple. God has a limit when you start messing with His holiness.

Fast forward through the first chapters of Ezekiel which deal with the judgment of the Israelites, past the second section which covers judgment for other nations, to the third section...restoration.

Beginning in chapter 40, Ezekiel is given a vision for a restored Temple of God, a temple that has yet to be built. This is one of those sections that we have a tendency to speed read or skip altogether. It is verse after verse of measurements for this restored Temple. Section by section, room by room the Temple is described...the Outer Courts, the North Gate, the South Gate, the Chambers for the Priests, the Inner Courts... the kind of details that usually make my eyes glaze over.

Here's an artist's drawing of what is described to Ezekiel. In the center of the temple is the Most Holy Place, the Holy of Holies. It housed the Ark of the Covenant, which represented the presence of God.

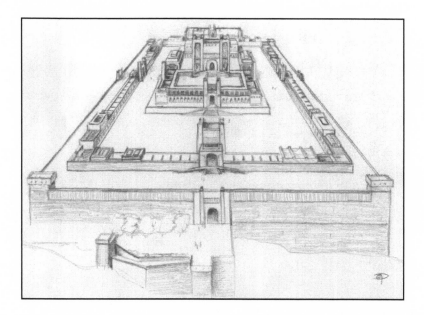

In ancient times the only person who could enter the Holy of Holies was the high priest, and then only once a year. They would tie a rope around the high priest's ankle, just in case there was some sin in his life that was offensive to God, so they could pull him out if he was zapped dead. The Holy of Holies was set apart from the rest of the Temple.

You'll notice the temple is square. Ezekiel 42:20 tells us

that each side is 500 cubits, which is about 875 feet, and that the outer walls separate the holy from the common. If the Holy of Holies is pure white, the rest of the Temple is maybe some shade darker, but still holy, and set apart from the common surroundings.

But it doesn't stop there. Ezekiel 45:1 tells us that when they build this temple, they are to set aside a sacred space, or a holy district, for God that is about seven miles long by six miles wide. It's not a wildlife refuge or peaceful sanctuary where nothing ever happens; it is set aside for the priests and their families, those who were called to be intentional about holiness.

It's important to note here that just because one section might not be as holy as the next, that doesn't mean that it is unholy. God makes a distinction here between holiness and the common, but never says that the common is unholy. Living a life of holiness is never common or ordinary, even in the midst of common surroundings.

If you were to Google Earth the Temple Mount in Jerusalem, you'd see a picture of what it looks like today. Of course, there is no Temple because it was destroyed in 70 A.D. But you could see the Islamic Dome of the Rock sharing the 35 acres that make up the Temple Mount.

In contrast to those 35 acres, Ezekiel's future holy space around the Temple will be 26,880 acres. The holy district that God demands the Temple to be surrounded with is forty-two square miles. Again, set apart. Obviously not as holy as the Holy of Holies, nor as holy as the Temple proper (since it was described as common), but still set apart... another shade of gray.

What we begin to see is the requirement that any place God dwells should have a holiness border that radiates from the center, extending out beyond what we can see. On level ground the average-sized person can see about three miles. It's interesting, isn't it, that God doesn't even want to see unholiness from afar.

Let's take a few moments and think of our lives in these same concentric circles. Today, the Holy of Holies resides in us. We have the presence of God wherever we go. In this zone, God's presence still requires set-apartness. At the core of our character our unsanctified imaginations allow bitterness, envy, lust, apathy, pride, selfishness, the lack of love and many other things to take root in dark recesses where they can grow and fester until they take over completely. God will not force His way around in there.

If you feed the darkness, or the shade of grayness, God will let you have your way...along with all of the consequences of your decisions. Although He will never abandon your Holy Temple like He did the Israelite's in Ezekiel's day. Love never demands its way.

Proverbs 4:23 says,

"23...guard your heart for it is the wellspring of life." [NIV]

To guard is not a passive activity. We must be proactive, watchful, vigilant, and alert. The Apostle Paul says in Philippians 4:8:

"8Finally, brothers, whatever is true, whatever is noble, whatever is right, whatever is pure, whatever is lovely, whatever is admirable--if anything is excellent or praiseworthy--think about such things." [NIV]

These things invite God into the conversation in your heart, and increase holiness. But they require our initiative.

Notice that neither of these verses focuses on saying "no" to sin. You can't say "no" to sin for very long. The moment you make sin the focus, it takes root and begins to grow. Instead, a life of holiness practices saying "yes" to the things of God.

The next circle out represents those things we do in His name. It includes our ministry both public and private. It is here that we are prone to allow our agendas to pollute and diminish the cause of Christ. We can cause disunity in the church. We care more about being right than about the preservation of relationships. It's here we forget that people are the product of discipleship, not a means to accomplish our task list. People are never disposable, never a means to an end, they are the end from God's perspective.

It is here where Paul's words, from Philippians 4 should guide us,

> *"³Do nothing out of selfish ambition or vain conceit, but in humility consider others better than yourselves. ⁴Each of you should look not only to your own interests, but also to the interests of others."* Philippians 4:3-4 [NIV]

And, in 1 John 3:

> *"[18]Dear children, let us not love with words or tongue but with actions and in truth. [19]This then is how we know that we belong to the truth, and how we set our hearts at rest in his presence [20]whenever our hearts condemn us."* 1 John 3:18-20 [NIV]

When we love the way Christ loves, it impacts our hearts.

The next circle represents the rest of our lives. Like God, we should desire to keep unholiness farther away than the human eye can see. Which, frankly, is hard to do in our sin-saturated culture. We're surrounded on every side.

But it is here, in these everyday places, that we tend to compartmentalize our lives and buy into the lie that what we do at work or at home doesn't impact our Christianity. It shows up in how we drive, how we act, and how we talk; it's revealed in how we treat people at work, at home or at the store.

First Timothy tells us that the overseer's life should be above reproach. The movies we watch, the TV shows that capture our interest, the way we approach our work, the way we conduct ourselves at home and in public, the language we use, the way we interact with those of the opposite gender...even the way we drive...all of these should be above reproach at all times. You should build the kind of reputation that protects you from all slander and accusation.

If we allow sin to encroach here, it will overtake the rest of our lives 5 mph at a time, until at our very core, the place where God dwells is surrounded by the darkness of our sin. In fact, we become like the Israelites. In Ezekiel 43:8, God says,

> *"⁸When they set up their worship shrines right alongside mine with only a thin wall between them, they dragged my holy name through the mud with their obscene and vile worship. Is it any wonder that I destroyed them in anger?"* [The Message]

We allow the wall between His shrine in our hearts to become too thin and drag His holy name through the mud.

No matter how well we think we can guard our hearts, we aren't strong enough to stand the continual assault if we allow unholiness to encroach our borders. Keep sin as far away as you can. Build solid boundaries to guide you when temptation comes your way.

Though, from our perspective, we will never truly be holy until that day we cross the finish line, our lives should be in constant movement toward that end. Worship is slow obedience in a God-ward direction. You might even call it a holy obsession.

Thoughts for Reflection:

1. What does it mean to say "yes" to the things of God versus "no" to sin?

2. Are you in a situation where relationship needs to trump being right?

3. Do you compartmentalize your life into work, ministry, home, etc.?

4. What does it mean to live above reproach? Is there anything in your life that is not above reproach?

5. How can/will you build solid boundaries to guide when temptation comes your way?

Chapter 7

Worship
is a Choice.

W HEN I WAS IN COLLEGE, I had the "privilege" one
summer of washing dishes at a church camp. Six
days a week...fourteen hours a day...scalding hot water.
Sometimes I was sure the cooks let the edges of the lasagna
burn just so I'd get to scrub a little harder.

After a couple of weeks, I have to admit my attitude stunk
a little...well, a lot really. I was making myself miserable. You
know how it happens, you start feeling sorry for yourself
and everything just goes downhill from there. I hated to get
up in the morning. I was whiny. I figured if I was going to be
miserable everyone else should be as well. I'm sure I was a
joy to work with.

One Sunday morning I was sitting in church feeling

sorry for myself...not paying attention to the speaker... which, by the way, is never OK. You should always pay close attention to the speaker! I found myself praying something like this "God you've brought me to this place. I hate what I'm doing. I'm miserable. It's your responsibility to make it all better." Yeah, my attitude was *God's fault.*

The good news is that God's shoulders are big enough to handle our blame, and often He turns the end of our rope into a lifeline.

I started leafing through my Bible, scanning a couple of Psalms that caught my eye, when the lyrics to a song just popped off the page. After church, before I was scheduled to start washing dishes again, I sat down at a piano and put a melody to the words.

> *"Make a joyful shout to God,*
> *All the earth rejoice.*
> *Sing out the honor of His name.*
> *Make His praise glorious*
> *Say to God,*
> *"How awesome are Your works*
> *Through the greatness of His holiness."*

"Sing to God,

Sing praises to His holy name.

Praise Him above the clouds by His name.

Rejoice forevermore before His throne.

Sing to God."

I can honestly say that the words are truly a work of art, because I didn't write them…David did. I just pulled them out of the Psalms. So I feel pretty confident in saying look at how he modeled worship. All of these phrases are action phrases. Make a choice to worship. Sing. Shout. Praise. Rejoice. David is saying "just do it."

So that's what I did. I started singing this very personal worship song while I did the dishes. As soon as I took my eyes off of myself and put them where they belonged…on Him, my entire perspective changed. Every time I washed a dish, I was worshipping.

Long before David was king, he too drew the short straw when it came to household chores. He led an unremarkable life. He was a small town boy, born and raised in a rural part of the country. As the eighth son of a rancher, he received all of the leftover genes. His brothers were big and strong. He seemed destined to be both small and forgotten.

David spent most of his time out on the range. He would

often sleep out under the stars while watching over the herds, seemingly content with his lot in life. He went about the task fearlessly, protecting the animals from whatever danger might come their way.

2 Chronicles 16:9 says,

"⁹The eyes of the Lord search the whole earth in order to strengthen those whose hearts are fully committed to him." [NLT]

As He searched, He found David. And out there under the stars, God took David and began to shape him into a man of faith and action. His character was developed as he was mentored by the Spirit of God.

David's life changed in a moment.

The prophet Samuel was sent by God to David's small town of Bethlehem. Though no one else knew, Samuel knew that he would be anointing a son of Jesse as the next king. Telling the townspeople that he had come to sacrifice to the Lord, he invited them to join him for the sacrifice.

As Samuel looked over Eliab, the firstborn of Jesse, he thought, "What a fine choice." But God corrected and reminded Samuel that He doesn't look at outward appearances, but at a man's heart. God rejected each of Jesse's sons until, prompted by Samuel, they ran to the fields to get their forgotten David.

Nothing immediately changed for David. He didn't become king overnight. But a divine plan was put into motion. David began to work his way up the ranks...serving as King Saul's musician, killing the giant Goliath, and later becoming a general in the army where he was loved by everyone, even more than the king.

King Saul became jealous of the attention lavished upon David, and as a result, David spent the last years of Saul's life on the run. It wasn't until Saul died in battle that David became king.

Throughout his lifetime, David was a poet and musician, writing at least 73 of the songs that make up the 150 songs in the book of Psalms. He is certainly the most famous worshiper of all time, known for some incredible highs in his life and some devastating failures. In spite of these failures, David is described as "a man after God's own heart." God recognized him as a worshiper.

But, one of David's failures cost him the life of his son.

This story of David begins in 2 Samuel 11. We find that David sent his army into battle, but he himself has stayed in Jerusalem. He got up from a nap one afternoon, and walking out onto the balcony, lo and behold, he saw a

beautiful woman bathing. After he picked his jaw up from ·
the floor, he found out she was Bathsheba, the wife of Uriah,
one of his loyal fighters.

We don't know how long it took, but at some point,
David sent someone to get Bathsheba. She came to the
palace and he slept with her. The next thing you know, she
was pregnant. Then, David panicked. He turned his back
on his integrity and decided to cover it up.

His plan was pretty simple. He sent for Uriah and
asked for an update on the battle front, before sending him
home to his wife for the night. You know what David was
thinking... husband sees wife he misses very much, they
share a blessed reunion. Uriah would never know that she
was already pregnant.

But Uriah can't imagine enjoying the comforts of home
while his brothers-in-arms are still fighting. So, he slept at
the palace. In the morning, when David found out, he went
to Plan B. He got Uriah drunk and sent him home. Again, no
go.

So David stooped to one of the lowest points of his life.
He wrote his general a note and Uriah carried his own
death warrant back to the battle field. The general read it,
followed the order, and Uriah died.

And, David married Bathsheba. Whew! He covered it up….no one would ever know.

But God is not pleased. So He sent the prophet Nathan to David to hold him accountable. He called David on his junk, and David suddenly got it. "I've sinned against God." He was repentant.

God loves a repentant heart, but there are still consequences for our sin. So God allowed David to live, because God forgives. But the consequence of his sin meant that the son born to Bathsheba would die.

David prayed desperately for God to change His mind. He fasted and slept on the floor, refusing to leave the baby's room. But God still took the baby's life. Sin is serious to God, especially the sin of one of His leaders.

As soon as David realized his son had died, he got up, washed his face, combed his hair, changed clothes and – get this – went to worship.

I think this story is incredible. It tells us so much about David, about God and about worship.

Worship is a choice we make regardless of our circumstances or feelings.

I suspect that our struggle with this concept isn't a principled one – we know in our hearts that this is true. I suspect that the root of our struggle is a control issue, an unwillingness to surrender.

We like the good, but not the bad. We want the highs, but not the lows. We want life to be a bed of roses with no thorns. Unfortunately our lives are filled with bad and lows and thorns. Our lives are filled with...well...dirty dishes.

We struggle to make ends meet. Our children have minds of their own and make choices that hurt them and their future. We lose our jobs, our marriages, our health, and like David, our loved ones. We live in conflict.

On top of the struggles, we are so busy *doing* that we erase all of the margin in our lives and have a hard time enjoying *being*. We're too tired, and every Monday we jump back on the merry-go-round for another seven days.

Frankly, we don't *feel* like worshiping.

David was in mourning. He didn't feel like worshiping. He probably felt guilty; after all it was his sin that led to the baby's death. But he chose to worship. God revealed His righteousness, justice and mercy to David.

And David chose to worship Him because of those character traits, not in spite of them. He chose to celebrate that the God he serves is righteous and just and merciful. He could have chosen to turn his back on God.

It's easy to worship when life is good. There is nothing like a mountain top experience with God. And, who wouldn't want more of them? Yet, we only recognize mountain tops because we've been in the valley.

What could our lives look like if we figured out how to make every moment a moment of worship?

Regardless of the circumstances we face in our lives, when we choose to worship in the midst of the storm, we are saying, "I trust You, God. I know that You are good, and You have a plan and a purpose for my life."

If we can't worship Him when things in our lives are at their worst, how can our worship mean anything when our circumstances are at their best? He is still God, and in control in both situations.

A few years ago someone I trusted greatly betrayed that trust in a big way. The result of his betrayal was like a knife to my heart. My heart hurt worse than I can ever remember, and I was ready to walk away from leading worship. I was questioning my calling.

I remember going home to DeeDee, wondering how I was going to lead my wife through this valley. I turned to the best source of wisdom I know, my Bible, and God led me to Hebrews 4.

"12For the word of God is full of living power. It is sharper than the sharpest knife, cutting deep into our innermost thoughts and desires. It exposes us for what we really are. 13Nothing in all creation can hide from him. Everything is naked and exposed before his eyes. This is the God to whom we must explain all that we have done." Hebrews 4:12-13 [NLT]

I knew in that moment that every trial I had ever faced had prepared me for this moment. I could respond by trusting God or I could lash out in my hurt. I knew that when my heart was laid bare before Him that I wanted Him to see that I chose to worship. The story of how God restored my heart is quite amazing.

Making this kind of choice isn't easy. Trusting in the sovereignty of God generally takes practice, and usually comes after failing, time and time again. But every time I've failed, I've gotten back up and tried again. Every day is filled with opportunities to practice choosing a life of worship.

What will you choose?

Thoughts for Reflection:

1. Are you experiencing a situation where you need to make a choice to worship?

2. What does God see when He looks at your heart?

3. Pray that God would reveal anything in your life that you are unwilling to surrender.

4. Are you so busy "doing" that you aren't spending enough time "being"?

5. What is a recent "mountain top" experience for you? What is a recent valley? How has God proved faithful to you through those experiences?

Chapter 8

Worship
has an Audience of One.

I WAS TEN WHEN I WAS INTRODUCED to the stage as a form of communication. I was the nerdy fifth grade student who actually liked helping out in the library at school. One day I found a shelf of plays and started reading. I found one in particular that I liked, and somehow convinced my teacher and the school administration to let me cast (including myself in the starring role), produce and direct this great work of art.

From a fifth grader's perspective it was a work of art (though I'm sure it was quite painful for anyone of adult age), but acting really wasn't my thing, so I moved on to music. Guitar lessons led to teaching myself how to play the piano, which was made possible by a first period choir class because we didn't have a piano at home. The rest is, as they say, history.

Since those early years, I have sung thousands of songs on hundreds of stages, with musicians of every caliber.

Maybe it's because I've worked so closely with musicians and speakers, both on and off the stage, that I have never thought of them as anything but normal people (well...normal might be questionable). What I mean is that regardless of any fame or stature, I don't put any of them on a pedestal. I'm not star-struck, and am surprised sometimes when someone else is, especially when they are star-struck about me.

I was in Italy on a mission trip. Five lovely weeks in what is affectionately called the "arm pit" of Italy, Naples. In reality, there are some very beautiful areas and the people more than make up for any part that may be arm-pitish.

In my role, I wasn't representing my church directly, but DELTA Ministries International (the finest short-term missions organization in the world, I might add). However, some members of my church were also on the team.

One day I sat down to lunch with them. It was rare to have a moment to relax so I wanted to touch bases and see how they were doing away from home. Timmie was at the table, someone I'd seen at church, but never met.

Lunch was great, the conversation engaging. But it was at the end that Timmie caught me by surprise. She said, "Chris, I'm so glad you came to sit with us. I've wanted to talk to you so many times when I've passed you in the halls at church. But every time I stop myself because you are so beyond me."

Clearly, the platform I sang from regularly had become, for Timmie, a pedestal that she put me on every day.

I couldn't help myself. I laughed at her, and then said, "Timmie, I put my pants on one leg at a time, just like everyone else."

We live in a culture that loves to put people on a pedestal. We are looking for heroes. Looking to lift ourselves out of the daily quagmire in which we live. We live vicariously through the lives of the rich and famous, and find ourselves wanting to brush shoulders with anyone "famous", even if their fame is nebulous at best. When I was in college, I actually touched Amy Grant's hand while she sang on stage at one of her concerts....ooooh.

And then, when our "heroes" don't live up to our expectations, we love to tear them down, dissecting their lives along with every decision they've ever made, and judging them so we feel better about ourselves.

Whether we live our lives on a stage or off, it's easy to fall into the trap of doing whatever it is that we do to impress or please others; or, to keep them from judging us.

Authentic worship only cares about the opinion of ONE.

Worship doesn't work this way. Authentic worship doesn't care about the opinions of others. Authentic worship only cares about the opinion of ONE.

As you'll remember from chapter two, the Ark of the Covenant still hadn't made its trek to the City of David, Jerusalem. After Uzzah-gate, David, in his anger (and fear) toward God, decided to sideline the Ark in the household of Obed-Edom. For three months, the presence of God totally blessed the house of Obed-Edom.

Now David, who was just like us, decided he wanted a piece of the action. So he went out to try once more to bring the Ark to Jerusalem.

Again, lots of people, big party. They were dancing their way back to Jerusalem with David in the lead, celebrating with wild abandon before God.

A common misconception is that David danced in his

underwear, or maybe even naked. I was once told of a worship team who decided to rehearse like David danced. I'm not sure what they were thinking, and neither was the person who caught them. It was their last rehearsal as a worship team.

David was clothed. He wore a linen ephod which was clothing that the priests wore. The point of this passage isn't what David wore, but what he *didn't*. He set aside his royal robes and acted like a commoner. He wasn't concerned about his position. He wasn't concerned about what other people thought. In fact, he was acting just like everyone else.

As they arrived in the city, David's wife Michal heard the ruckus, and looked out her window. She saw David leaping and doing the Ark of the Covenant shuffle before God, and her heart was filled with contempt for him. In her mind, his actions were beneath his position.

He finished up the day, headed home, and found her waiting to greet him. Her voice dripped with sarcasm as she said,

> "[20]*How wonderfully the king has distinguished himself today...exposing himself to the eyes of*

the servant's maids like some burlesque street dancer." 2 Samuel 6:20 [The Message]

His response:

"In God's presence I'll dance all I want! He chose me over your father and the rest of our family and made me prince over God's people, over Israel. Oh yes, I'll dance to God's glory - more recklessly even than this. And as far as I'm concerned . . . I'll gladly look like a fool . . . but among these maids you're so worried about, I'll be honored no end." vs. 22-23 [The Message]

God must have agreed with David, because Michal was barren the rest of her life.

When we worship, God is the sole audience.

But the story doesn't end there. When the Ark was finally established in Jerusalem, David gathered the people of Israel to celebrate the presence of God in Jerusalem. It was another great party.

> When we worship, God is the sole audience.

And, when the festivities were over and everyone had

gone home, he appointed the Levite (priestly) musicians to minister regularly before the Ark. Let that sink in a moment.

There were no regular church services happening in Jerusalem at this time. When Israel wanted to offer a sacrifice of worship, they would go to Gibeon. That means, most of the time it was just the musicians – singing, playing, dancing – worshiping in the presence of God. He was the only audience.

Whether we are in a church service, worshiping with hundreds of people, or cleaning the house alone, if it is worship, God is always the only audience.

And since "the show" which is our lives always has a sold-out audience, we should incorporate the principles of David's worship into our own.

First, David's reckless worship was motivated by gratitude for all that God had done for him. He recognized the incredible privilege of being chosen to be king by the Creator. He could have been left out in the fields tending sheep, all but forgotten by his family. But God plucked him out of the pasture and dropped him into a palace.

We too have been chosen by the Creator, and have become royalty (see Ephesians 1:5-6). He could have left us, forgotten, out in the pasture. Though some of us keep trying to return there, it is no longer our home.

The amazing grace we have received has washed us clean and set us on a new path, one that will lead to an eternal relationship with the God who took extreme measures to make it possible. We are not the same, but now have the Living God, literally residing in us, giving us the power to walk this new path.

We have much for which to be thankful.

We live in the richest, most advanced country in the world. If you earn more than $10,000 per year, you rank in the top 10 percent of the wealthiest people globally. We have running water, reliable electricity, hot showers, enough food to waste and movies on demand.

If that's not enough for you, you're breathing aren't you? What more do you need? You don't deserve any of this. Count your blessings and remember their source.

Second, David also recognized that his calling to be a worshiper trumped his position as a king. He understood that what he *did* was less important than who he was. God didn't need David to be King. He could easily find someone else. After all, He easily found David when Saul, Israel's first king, forgot this principle.

David was a worshiper when he was alone with the

sheep, enjoying the presence of God under the stars. David was a worshiper when he stood before Goliath with five smooth stones. David was a worshiper when he crouched in a cave while his king, Saul, took a moment to relieve himself and David spared his life. David was a worshiper regardless of his circumstances, sometimes in spite of them.

> God calls us to be with Him. God wants us to *be* worshipers, people who orient their lives to His presence.

Like David, our calling as worshipers trumps all else. We have a tendency to elevate what we do for God over who we are with God. God doesn't need us to do anything for Him. Our circumstances are just tools He uses to disciple us. God calls us to be with Him. God wants us to *be* worshipers, people who orient their lives to His presence.

When we reverse the order we become like Michal, David's wife. We watch worship happen somewhere else – with someone else – judging their performance. We stand on the sidelines while worship happens around us, never experiencing God as He designed.

Third, David's reckless worship was motivated by the

desire to be in God's presence. David's entire life was a testament to this principle, let alone this particular passage. David could have watched the parade from afar with his wife, Michal. He could have ridden in the royal carriage and overseen a more sober procession.

But worship from afar was never David's choice. He liked to get down and dirty (in all the right ways) when it came to God's presence. Given the chance, he would have been wrestling God like Jacob. It was David who would pen words of longing like:

> *"In your presence there is fullness of joy,"*

> *"As a deer pants for flowing streams, so pants my for soul for you, O God,"* and

> *"My soul longs, yes, faints for the courts of the Lord,"* Psalms 16:11; 42:1; 84:1 [NIV]

These aren't the words of a man who would ever worship from afar.

In God's presence, where we have no control, there is fullness of joy for us as well. There is freedom. There is longing. There is peace. There is celebration. In God's presence, no one else's opinion matters.

Yet, we generally like to keep God at arm's length. Giving up control is rather scary to most of us. So we go through our days, solving problems, making money, chasing kids (and sadly, for some, even going to church), with barely a thought that we always have an Audience. And our Audience wants the "show" to be interactive.

Just because we aren't aware of His presence doesn't make it less real. What will you do to be like David?

Thoughts for Reflection:

1. Is your current audience more than one? Who else might you be striving to please?

2. List 10 things for which you are thankful.

3. How can what we do become more important than who we are?

4. How might you be critical of others' worship?

5. What motivates your desire to worship?

6. Pray that God would reveal anything that may be hindering your worship.

Chapter 9

Worship
Loves Others

LIKE TOO MANY TEENAGERS, I entered adulthood with a pretty low self-esteem. The abuse that had been a part of my life since the age of three, combined with challenging middle and high school years, left me feeling pretty unlovable.

If I had known then, what I learned in my early thirties, my life would have looked a little different; though I'm not sure that it would have looked better.

Through my college years, then on through my twenties, I figured out subconsciously that if I could solve a person's problems they would "love" me. In my work place, in my churches, with my friends, I tried to become indispensable.

If someone had a computer problem, I would figure out

how to fix it...and be loved. When there was an unmet need at work, I would learn whatever I needed to learn so that I could stand in the gap. That's how I learned bookkeeping and payroll, human resources, marketing, graphic design and video editing. I was looking for love in all the wrong places.

Clearly it was an unhealthy, co-dependent way to find love. I should have read Ephesians and some of the Psalms a little more closely. God's Word definitely had the answers I was looking for (though I didn't understand it at the time).

It wasn't until I was 33 that a conversation with someone who was unhappy with me triggered an "a-ha" moment. I sat in my office with Karen, who was fighting someone else's battle. As she shared her heart, she wanted me to share more of mine in the larger context of our worship team.

I stared at her, with a confused look on my face, and told her I couldn't imagine that anyone would be interested in what was going on in my heart. She said, simply, "I think you're wrong. There are a lot of people who care."

Imagine that. Her simple comment changed the trajectory of my life.

But just like every coin has two sides, there is an upside

to my unhealthy search for love. I became a jack-of-all-trades (and definitely master-of-none). And, I learned early on what a life of serving others should look like.

I became a firefighter.

That's how I describe my role sometimes. I help solve people's problems. I fight fires. And here you thought I was just a worship pastor.

Every time someone walks through my door looking for help, I have an opportunity to be a blessing to them. No person who walks through my door looking for help is ever an interruption. They give me an opportunity to express worship in a tangible way. When we bless others, we bless God. When we bless God, its worship.

In the last week of Jesus' ministry on earth, He spent time at the Temple teaching, confounding and astounding any who listened. Even the leaders. Especially the leaders.

"34Hearing that Jesus had silenced the Sadducees, the Pharisees got together. 35One of them, an expert in the law, tested him with this question: 36'Teacher, which is the greatest commandment in the Law?' 37Jesus replied: 'Love the Lord your God with all your heart and with all your soul and with all your mind.' 38This is the first and greatest

*commandment. ³⁹And the second is like it: 'Love
your neighbor as yourself.' ⁴⁰All the Law and the
Prophets hang on these two commandments."*
Matthew 22:34-40 [NIV]

It was the normal practice of the rabbis to get together
to discuss the law. In fact, part of the education process for
those studying to become rabbis was to ask questions like
this, and then debate the answer.

I'm not sure that the question was designed to "catch"
Jesus, but would guess that they were hoping that the
ensuing discussion might trap Him.

Jesus' answer is not a surprise to them. But His meaning
is incredibly important for us to grasp. The first law He
mentions encompasses the heart of worship. Loving God
with every fiber of our physical, emotional, intellectual and
spiritual being is worship. No one in that context would
disagree with Him, in fact good Jews repeated this verse
(though from the Old Testament) twice a day.

But Jesus didn't stop there. From His vantage point
there isn't just one great commandment, but two. And the
second isn't of less importance than the first. It is equal.

Love your neighbor as yourself.

Let's see if we understand this correctly from Jesus'

perspective: if we love God, we will love others. When we love our others, we love God.

The reverse is also frighteningly true. When we don't love others, we don't love God. Yikes.

It would be easy if everyone were lovable. I can love the lovable. Too bad there are more than a few less than lovable people in our lives. You'd think God was testing us, to keep us growing or something.

Throughout His earthly ministry, Jesus had quite a bit to say about the type of relationships that we should have with one another. He called us to love our neighbors and our enemies. He taught us not to judge and how to treat those less fortunate than ourselves.

In one section of the Sermon on the Mount, found in Matthew 5, Jesus is recorded as saying this about retaliating when we've been wronged:

> "*38You have heard that it was said, 'Eye for eye, and tooth for tooth.' 39But I tell you, do not resist an evil person. If someone strikes you on the right cheek, turn to him the other also. 40And if someone wants to sue you and take your tunic, let him have your cloak as well. 41If someone forces you to go one mile, go with him two miles. 42Give to the one*

who asks you, and do not turn away from the one
who wants to borrow from you." Matthew 5:38-
42 [NIV]

In these few verses we find a principle that will help make our interactions with others an act of worship. Let's call it "The Extra Mile Principle."

There's nothing wrong with the first mile. In the first mile you are doing what's been asked of you. In the first mile you, at the very least, didn't refuse to go on the journey. In the first mile you are still serving someone.

Here's the problem with the first mile. In the first mile you can grumble, whine and complain. You can do the first mile with a rotten attitude. But, a rotten attitude steals any worship from the act. It's incredibly easy for the first mile to be wasted from a worship perspective.

BUT, the moment you step into the second mile you are in control of the heart of the deed. No longer are you doing what's been asked of you, but you have chosen to join someone on their journey, serving them as you walk along. In the extra mile, your heart becomes engaged in a God-honoring way.

In the extra mile you worship.

Here are some simple, practical ways this might look for us:

- You're walking down the hall at work; it's a busy day with many deadlines. You pass a coworker who says, "Hi." A first mile response returns the greeting and keeps on walking. The extra mile stops, makes eye contact with a smile and asks them about their day.

- You're driving in heavy traffic. That inconsiderate driver (there's always one you wish a policeman would get) rushes around you just so they can get back into your lane before the exit. *"Really? What's the time difference in one car length?"* you think. A first mile response lets them in, barely, grumbling all the while. The extra mile lets them in, praying that whatever situation has them frantic resolves itself to their blessing.

- The sink is full of dishes again. None of them are yours. To top things off, the dishwasher is full of clean dishes that need to be put away. Most of us are non-starters for this one. We never even step into the first mile. Those of us who do step up usually do so grumbling about the lack of consideration for all we do around the house. The extra mile puts an 'S' on the mile (smile) and sacrifices ten minutes for the rest of the family, who've been busy all day as well, praying for them while cleaning up.

In no way do I mean to trivialize any individual situation or excuse poor behavior on someone else's part. Nor do I mean to imply that you should become a door mat and allow bad behavior to continue (that isn't love by the way). My point here isn't about them. It's about you and how you make your interactions with others an act of worship.

God blesses the extra mile. He loves to inhabit the extra mile with you.

In her sophomore year in high school, my daughter, Lexi, tore the labrum in her shoulder in two places. It took months of doctor's appointments and physical therapy for the professionals to decide that she indeed needed surgery, followed by several more months of physical therapy.

Because my work schedule is incredibly flexible, it became my responsibility two or three times a week to ferry her from school to the appointment of the day. It was inconvenient and unproductive for me from a work perspective. It required hours of makeup time in the evening and on weekends.

A first mile approach could certainly get her from one place to another. But it could also make her feel guilty for being injured in the first place (which she didn't need any help feeling). It could also make her feel like my time was more valuable than hers by focusing on the interruption in my work flow.

I chose the extra mile approach. For months we had the privilege of riding together, waiting together, talking together, and laughing together. As a captive passenger in the car, she couldn't escape when I'd ask questions about her classes, her friends, her future.

At the end of the extra mile, our relationship was deeper than it had ever been (and it had always been great). She knew, more than ever, that her dad was on her side and would go to the mat for her. It broke down every wall that the typical teenager has with their parents.

God inhabits the extra mile.

Admittedly, going the extra mile is easy when the person on the receiving end is someone we love, or at least like. It is much harder when it is someone who drives us nuts. Unfortunately any lack of affection on our part doesn't let us off the hook. The context surrounding the extra mile principle in Jesus' teaching focuses on those who are less than easy to love.

> When we go the extra mile for anyone, especially someone who is challenging to serve, our light shines brighter.

My life verse is found in Matthew 5:15, "In the same way, let your light shine before men, that they may see your good deeds and praise your Father in heaven.

When we go the extra mile for anyone, especially someone who is challenging to serve, our light shines brighter. The brighter the light, the more glory to God. The more glory to God, the better the worship.

If we want our worship to shine, we must love the way Christ calls us to love, inhabiting the extra mile with Him.

Thoughts for Reflection:

1. In what ways are you a blessing to others?

2. What's one way that you can bless someone in your life that is difficult to love?

3. In which relationship or situation are you still in mile one?

4. What will it take to move you into the next mile?

Chapter 10

Worship
is a Lifestyle

I LOVE TO GIVE A GOOD GIFT. There's nothing like watching someone unwrap the perfect present for that moment in their lives.

A few years ago that perfect gift was for my son, Josh. As any 12-year-old with musical talents, he dreamt of the day he would be playing lead guitar in front of thousands. He started out happy with his acoustic guitar, but no kid ever dreams of playing acoustic guitar in a rock band. Strumming an acoustic guitar is just not as cool as ripping out an ear piercing solo on an electric guitar, with drums and bass in the background.

Being the kind of parents who want to be well-taken care of in our old age, we began looking for the perfect instrument, and amp, and strap, and case. We knew right away that our budget was going to ensure that our son would be asking for an electric guitar for many birthdays and Christmases to come.

If you look, you can find an electric guitar and amp as a set, from some of the retailers, for under $200. But you get what you pay for, and if your kid is serious about it, it won't be long before you are looking to upgrade. For the serious musician, upgrading your instrument is the same as upgrading your computer to a technogeek... neverending. There is always something bigger and better.

Our desperation led us to talk to our friend Stan. Stan is the ultimate guitarhead. He owns about 27 guitars. The ones he loves the most he's named. There is Lucille, a Gibson ES-345 B.B. King model; Lester, a deep burgundy, 1975 Les Paul; and, Ashley, a Telecaster that Stan lovingly crafted. (Ashley was going to be Woody until the first time I saw it and informed Stan that it was a girl.) You get the point. Stan loves everything electric guitar.

Stan not only loves playing electric guitar, but he loves it when others learn as well. Other players are not a threat to this humble musician, but become a part of his larger family. Over the years he has invested much of himself into helping fan the flames of passion for many a young guitar player. He has a big heart, and fortunately it was big enough for Josh.

With Stan's help we were able to get Josh a custom-built (by Stan) electric guitar, amp and all of the accessories at an unbelievably good price (meaning it cost Stan more than it cost us...thanks, friend).

So Christmas comes, and you can't just give the perfect gift in an ordinary way. As his last present, Josh opened a small box with a simple piece of paper in it, leading him on a scavenger hunt that ended with him finding his new electric guitar. My manly 12-year-old son screamed like a girl, bringing big smiles to our faces.

It was the *perfect* gift.

What gift would be perfect for the King of kings and Lord of lords? Not only does He own the cattle on a thousand hills, but He holds the universe in the palm of His hand. The streets of His city are paved with the purest of gold and the foundation, built on the finest of gemstones.

Our lives, on the other hand, are like a vapor or mist [see James 4:14]. What do we have that could possibly bless God? What could we offer that would capture His heart?

That's easy. Our lives.

As we've journeyed together, we've begun to understand that we were created to worship. We were created to connect with the God of the universe. And, for the most part, that connection has nothing to do with music.

It's about the way we live, day in and day out. It is a life wholly surrendered that pleases God.

Don't believe me? What about the Apostle Paul?

In Romans 12:1 he writes:

> *"¹Therefore, I urge you, brothers, in view of God's mercy, to offer your bodies as living sacrifices, holy and pleasing to God—this is your spiritual act of worship."* [NIV]

In the first eleven chapters of Romans, Paul spends a lot of time talking about the "mercy" of God. Chapter 12 is a transition in the book of Romans to the practical side of how we respond because of God's mercies. We see this in the very first word..."therefore." Because of God's mercies, it is now time for us to respond by doing something.

From Paul's perspective, God's mercy requires a response. You see this in the next phrase: I urge you. Because we're reading text on a page, we generally miss the emphasis Paul intended.

It's not 'urge' as in "if you get around to this," or "if you feel like it." The language is much stronger than that. Other translations say plead...beg...appeal. If this were an email to the church, Paul would have used all-caps, bold and italic to get his point across. *I URGE* you. This is something you must do in view of God's mercy. Mercy demands a response.

> ## Mercy demands a response.

And that response? Our bodies, offered as living sacrifices. This is in contrast to the sacrifices of the Old Testament. Before the sacrifice of Christ on the cross, God's mercy required the blood of a *dead* sacrifice. We get to be *live* sacrifices.

Paul is not telling us to be like the Jews in the Old Testament who offered the sacrifice in order to gain favor with God. Paul is telling us to be like the sacrifice. The Jews got off easy...they spent a few bucks. The sheep, their pathway is a little harder. It requires commitment to be a sheep of sacrifice.

In many ways we get off easy—compared to the sheep— but Paul is telling us that we should have the commitment of a sheep. Sacrifice is essential to worship.

And, just as the Israelites couldn't offer any old sheep, but only the best, our living sacrifice must be our best. It must be holy and pleasing to God. If we want to capture the heart of God, we must embrace the things of God.

> **If we want to capture the heart of God, we must embrace the things of God.**

I've been a Christian for more than 35 years now, which is clearly longer than I've been alive (joking). And in 35 years, I can honestly tell you that this is easier said than done. And I know that I am not alone. In just the last few months, as a pastor, I've talked with people who have had their marriages rocked by affairs, or marriages just plain old falling apart. I've talked with people who struggle with pornography, workaholism, abuse, addiction, financial chaos...you name it. And these people are Christians, just like you and me!

We all have the best of intentions. We want to be godly men and women. We want to do what's right. We want to spend time reading our Bibles, praying, memorizing, and meditating. We want to encourage one another and build each other up. The problem is that, even though we are new creations we still live in a fallen world with fallen bodies.

I was talking to someone struggling with an addiction not too long ago. I asked him "How long have you been trying to stop?" His answer...five years! "Has anything worked?" Obviously not. So, either there is no hope or he has to change his paradigm—the way he thinks—and try it a different way.

After eons of trying, I've figured out that Chris Voigt, in and of himself, has no power to embrace the things of God. Holiness is not a part of my natural self. I desire it, but I can't get there on my own steam. We need help for this journey.

So the first part of embracing the things of God is having the wisdom and humility to ask for His help. An honest heart, seeking after God, will always find Him. He isn't out there playing a game of cosmic hide and seek. He wants to

> An honest heart, seeking after God, will always find Him.

be found! Then, the more you move toward God, the more you want to move toward God.

That's what made King David "a man after God's own heart." It wasn't that he never sinned. He was a lying, adulterous, murderer whose sin of pride caused the deaths of seventy thousand people. And yet, God still called him "a man after God's own heart." His secret...he never let his sin get in the way of his relationship with God.

Like Paul, he understood that worship is first and foremost a spiritual act, before it is a physical act. It emanates from the inside out. It's not about what we *do*, it's about who we *are*.

Worship begins and ends with the heart. We can become the greatest servants in the world, but apart from Christ, our actions don't make us worshipers. They make us great servants. We can know more about God than anyone else, but apart from Christ, we just have lots of knowledge. It isn't worship if our heart isn't in the right place.

Fortunately Paul continues in verse two to tell us how to become living sacrifices.

> *"²Do not conform any longer to the pattern of this world, but be transformed by the renewing of your mind. Then you will be able to test and approve what God's will is--His good, pleasing and perfect will."* Romans 12:2 [NIV]

Step one is to stop doing things the world's way.

We spend much of our lives just trying to fit in. It begins early. We don't want to be the last one picked for a team in P.E. class. We don't necessarily want to be popular, just not the butt of every joke, or any joke.

As we become adults we want to be like our friends. We feel the need to keep up with the Jones'. Our culture shoves its definition of success down our throats so we work harder and longer to buy bigger houses and better cars. We search for satisfaction in all the wrong places, never finding any sort of contentment.

This is what Paul is telling us to resist. He is saying, "Keep your perspective. Life is short. Eternity is long." We are called to be aliens in this world...in the world, not of it... salt and light. Nothing in this world will pass into eternity, EXCEPT our worship. In fact, you could look at our worship now as a training ground for eternity.

One of my favorite authors is Randy Alcorn, who leads Eternal Perspectives Ministries in Gresham, Oregon. The message of his book "The Edge of Eternity" is that we are becoming today what we will be in eternity. We have the freedom today to impact and change what eternity looks like for each of us, in a way that we won't have once we arrive on the other side of time. What do you want your eternity to look like?

Allow me to let you in on a little secret: If it makes sense from the world's perspective, RUN!

It's not enough to resist. We must allow God to transform our minds.

Transformation is a life-long process. We transform one godly decision at a time, each decision building upon the last. There is no Staples Easy-Button, no Disneyland Fast Pass.

We have become so indoctrinated into the things of the world that it takes time to rid ourselves of the junk.

As we submit to His leadership in our life, He does the transforming work. That's why we've been given the gift of the Holy Spirit, to do the transforming work, which is great because we don't have it in ourselves to do it any other way.

Puritan Pastor Richard Baxter (who died in 1691) prayed "May the Living God, who is the portion and rest of the saints, make these our carnal minds so spiritual, and our earthly hearts so heavenly, that loving Him, and delighting in Him, may be the work of our lives."

Paul ends with a promise. If you do all of the above, you will know the will of God. How many times have we wondered...what is God's will for me? How can I know? Here's the promise...if you live a life of worship you will know the will of God.

Now that we've worked our way through these two

verses in the New International Version, let's take a look at them in The Message.. I love the way it puts them.

> *"¹So here's what I want you to do, God helping you: Take your everyday, ordinary life—your sleeping, eating, going-to-work, and walking-around life— and place it before God as an offering. Embracing what God does for you is the best thing you can do for him. ²Don't become so well-adjusted to your culture that you fit into it without even thinking. Instead, fix your attention on God. You'll be changed from the inside out. Readily recognize what he wants from you, and quickly respond to it. Unlike the culture around you, always dragging you down to its level of immaturity, God brings the best out of you, develops well-formed maturity in you."* Romans 12:1-2 [The Message]

May your everyday, ordinary life be pleasing to Him.

Thoughts for Reflection:

1. How are you giving your body as a living sacrifice?

2. How is sacrifice the key to worship?

3. What is one way you can move toward God today?

4. Where do you most often search for contentment?

5. What part of your mind needs to be transformed by God? Are you willing to let Him?

Chris Voigt has been Pastor of Celebration Ministries at Dayspring Fellowship in Keizer, Oregon for 12 years and a lead worshipper for more than 20. He also contributes his time and seemingly boundless energy and talent to leading the Board of Directors of Worship Northwest, a growing ministry focused on building, equipping and encouraging lead worshippers in the local church.

Chris says, *"As a worship leader for more than 20 years, I have seen my share of healthy and unhealthy ministries. Through it all God has developed a desire in me to help other worship leaders build healthy, fully-functioning ministries; to help all believers love God with all of their heart, soul, mind and strength; to help churches become worshiping churches."*

Chris is an innovator and organizer, passionate and purposeful - a servant leader with a shepherd's heart. His fervent desire is to equip and challenge believers toward a lifestyle of worship.

Chris also serves on the Boards of Friends of Hope, and Extra Mile Media and has served as Chairman of the Board of DELTA Ministries International. In his spare time he does business consulting through his company Outsource Oregon. He plays keyboards and guitar (though he doesn't claim guitar very often), acknowledges an addiction to Diet Coke, and is husband to DeeDee and dad to two incredible teenagers, Lexi and Josh. You can find him online at www.chrisvoigtworship.com.

For booking information: lori@chrisvoigtworship.com